Disclaimer

The information included in this book is designed to provide helpful information on the subjects discussed. This book is not meant to be used to diagnose or treat any medical condition. For diagnosis or treatment of any medical problem, consult your own doctor. The author and publisher are not responsible for any specific health or allergy needs that may require medical supervision and are not liable for any damages or negative consequences from any application, action, treatment, or preparation, to anyone reading or following the information in this book. Links may change and any references included are provided for informational purposes only.

Family Games

Fun Games To Play With Family and Friends

By Susan Hollister

Table of Contents

Introduction

I want to thank you and congratulate you for getting this book filled with lots of games and fun ways to pass the time. Some games will keep you entertained for hours while others are the most fun when you play them with friends and loved ones.

The selection of games is endless! Today, most people play games on their cell phones, tablets and computers as well as using commercial video game consoles. While these games are good enough when you're in the mood to do something by yourself or with a friend or two, they aren't very useful when you're hosting a bunch of people or if you want to spend some quality bonding time with your friends and family.

Many traditional games do not require computer technology and they cost little to no money. You can play an endless variety of games using things you already have lying around your house – string, umbrellas, drinking straws, etc. You can make use of your tile floor, your stairway, even your walls – without damaging them, of course.

In this book you'll be exposed to a broad variety of games with basic instructions for their implementation, but don't let that stop you from making up your own rules! The most important thing for you to bring to the table is your imagination; that, and a desire to make some amazing memories with your friends and family.

Games do good things for children and adults alike. Not only do they provide hours of entertainment, many of the games listed in this book can help children build and reinforce crucial skills. These games can help people of all ages improve their focus and attention skills. Some will strengthen planning and prioritization, problem solving, or memorization.

When you spend time playing games with your family you are building confidence into your children, you are helping them develop communication skills and you are developing in them the ability to effectively interact with others. These things may not be taught in school but they are essential for living a meaningful life!

Adults also benefit greatly from playing games. We can take life so seriously! We, of all people, need to make periodic space in our lives to goof off and have some fun! Playing games, whether by yourself or with other people, can help you release stress, relax a tense mind and body, and can even sharpen your ability to think, all in the name of fun. If you need more convincing, watch the YouTube video entitled <u>Importance of Play</u> by RowanUniversity.

This book contains proven steps and strategies for playing games that are best suited for families and children. Each chapter of this book covers a specific category of games, making it easier to find a game that meets your specific needs. You will discover a broad variety of outdoor games that will have your children practically begging you to let them play in the yard whenever the sun's up. You will also discover some of the best games to play indoors when the weather is less than cooperative. These games are sure to entertain your children for hours and provide an effective antidote to the common rainy-day chorus of, "I'm bored!"

You can even join in on the fun if you are bored yourself. The majority of this book focuses on group games and activities you can use at large events, such as family reunions, BBQs, get-togethers, children's parties, school fairs and your very own family game night.

Starting a family game night in your home is very worthwhile! It is ideal to pick a pre-determined date, time and location to hold your game night so that everyone in your family can arrange around school and plan to be there. Announcing the time, date and location can be as simple as discussing it over dinner or announcing it on Facebook by creating a private event notice where you invite each individual family member.

You can make every game night different by giving it a creative and customized twist. One twist is to use a different theme each time and integrate snacks, music and decorations to go along with the theme. Another fun variation is to choose a different type of game each time. For example, one week you could play all imagination games, the next week you could play a variety of card and dice games. The week after that could be devoted to traditional board games.

Sharing the responsibility of setting up each family game night can also be a great opportunity to teach younger kids about planning and management skills. You can let them help by picking out themes, choosing which games to play and by giving them the responsibility of communicating the details to other members of your family. The best place to start learning how to set up a family game night is to check out some of the best games found in this book.

Chapter 1: Go, Play Outside

The great outdoors gives children and adults alike the opportunity to have a great time while breathing deeply of fresh air and soaking in all the benefits of the sun. Unfortunately, entire generations of children have moved most of their playtime indoors, focusing on computers, television, and video games. Research shows that the typical American child spends only one half hour in outside play – a stark contrast to previous generations who would often spend all day outside.

As a child, I used to love to play outside! I'd be up and out by 7:30 in the morning. Sometimes I'd stay out all day, only going inside the house for meals. When a friend was with me, we would spend endless hours in outdoor entertainment. If we tired of the games we knew, we'd make up our own.

Even when I was on my own, I would find something enjoyable to do outdoors. In this chapter, you will discover some of the best outdoor games.

Outdoor play can be just as much fun as playing inside. It offers many benefits because of the physical nature of most outdoor games. They can build cardiovascular strength and help fend off obesity. Spending time in the great outdoors increases your sun exposure, which is the best way to get Vitamin D, an essential element to boost your mood and ward off heart disease, diabetes and degenerative eye diseases. Outdoor play can help children develop gross motor skills, increase their balance, enhance their coordination, and build muscle strength.

Time outside is soothing to body, mind, and spirit. Research suggests that outdoor play can lessen the symptoms of ADHD. Schools with environmental-friendly programs have shown improvements in critical thinking and listening skills, and have reported better results on standardized tests. Research also suggests that playing freely in a green environment can reduce children's stress, anxiety, and depression levels.

Nature is a wonderful healer. When you are surrounded by trees, fresh air, songbirds, flowers, and other outdoor elements, you may find you have a more positive attitude, a stronger imagination, closer relationships, and improved social interactions. The Youtube video, <u>Benefits of Playing Outdoors: Let Kids Get Down and Dirty</u> by Kimberly Blaine describes additional benefits of playing outside.

Around the World

Number of players: 2 or more

In this basketball game, everyone takes turns shooting baskets from positions that circle around the basketball hoop. To move from one point to the next, players must successfully make the shot in their current position. When a player misses a shot, he or she gets one more chance to make it. The catch is, If the person misses again, that player must go back to the first spot and start over. I had lots of fun with this game growing up.

Ball Race

Number of players: 2 or more

For this fun racing game, you will need a large, open field, at least two players, and one soccer ball or kickball per player. The players start out together, side by side . The objective is to kick the ball to the finish line without crossing another player's ball. Whenever this happens the player must start again. The first player to kick their ball all the way past the finish line is the winner.

Classic Outdoor Sports

Number of players: 2 or more

Some of the most common outdoor activities are the classic sports. Basketball, soccer, kickball, tennis, dodgeball, whiffle ball, badminton, football, volleyball and hockey can all be adapted to meet your level of play and the shape and size of your playing field. Many stores sell equipment that allows you to play multiple sports using the same equipment, but you can also make do with what you have on hand. These classic sports are sure to entertain children for hours on end and can easily burn off all that excess energy.

Coin Toss

Number of players: 2 or more

This fun counting game requires a handful of change, a plastic container and a small kiddie pool. Prepare this game by filling a pool with water and then floating a plastic container in the pool. Have all players stand a couple feet away from the pool and divvy out the change evenly. The game consists of participants taking turns tossing a coin into the pool, with points awarded when they sink a coin into the container. Players keep track of their individual scores. Pennies count as one point, nickels are five points, etc. Whoever scores the highest number of points wins! You can make this game more challenging, or make it easier by changing the diameter size of the container.

Flashlight Tag

Number of players: 2 or more

This third twist of tag is best played in the dark. One player is picked to be "it" and holds a flashlight in hand. The other players must run away from the player who is "it." "It" tags other players by shining the flashlight beam on them. The last player standing becomes "it" for the next round.

Football Fortune

Number of players: 3 or more

Want to sharpen your math skills? This game requires a large open area, a football, and at least three players. It also helps to have someone who is willing to keep score. Prior to starting the game, all players must decide on a winning score value, and pick specific numbers that will cause players to lose all of their points along the way. One player throws the football and yells out a point value. The player who catches the ball wins that number of points. The first person to reach or exceed the winning number wins. Of course, if you catch the ball and your score adds up to a losing number, you lose all your points and must start over again.

Four Square

Number of players: 4 or more

Four square requires a minimum of four players, some chalk, a large ball, and a decent sized playing area. One player draws a large square and then draws two lines across the middle to make four smaller squares. Each player claims a square. Players then take turns hitting the ball into each other's squares. Players are eliminated when they are unable to hit the ball out of their square with their hands before it bounces a second time. The winner is the last one standing.

If there are more than four players, individuals can rotate into the game whenever a player is eliminated. The game continues until all the players have had a chance to play and everybody but one has been eliminated.

Freeze Tag

Number of players: 2 or more

In another fun twist of tag, one player is picked to be "it" and starts out by chasing the other players as they run away. When a player is tagged, he or she must stand still in a "frozen" position. The only way a player can can move again is to be tagged again by another player who is on the run. The game is over when all players are frozen.

Group Tag

Number of players: 2 or more

In this twist on the classic game of tag, one player is picked to be "it" and starts out by chasing the other players who run away. When a player is tagged, instead of sitting out, he or she joins the "it" player to chase the others. Every other player who is tagged does the same until there is a large group of children chasing only a few. The game is over when everyone is part of the group. The last person tagged can become the new "it" or you can use some other criterion for this selection.

Hide and Seek

Number of players: 2 or more

Hide and seek is a classic game that kids and adults of all ages can enjoy. This game can be played inside, but today we'll focus on the outdoor variety. Pick one player to be "it" and have that person count up to 30 while the rest of the players run off and hide. At the end of the count, the person who is "it" goes on the hunt for everyone who is hidden. Whoever is found last is the next person to be "it." For a fun variation, try playing in the dark. If you are playing this game outdoors, it is advisable to set safe boundaries so players can't wander into danger in the dark.

H-O-R-S-E

Number of players: 2 or more

If you have a basketball hoop, H-O-R-S-E can give you hours of fun. One player starts out by taking a shot. It can be an easy shot or it can be crazy difficult. If the player makes the shot, the other players have to attempt the exact same shot from the same location. When a player misses, he or she gets a letter, beginning with the "H" of "horse." When a player reaches the "E" of "horse", he or she is out of the game. The last player standing wins.

You can add interesting twists to this game, by shooting with one hand, standing on one leg, or by shooting with your back to the basket.

Jaws

Number of players: 3 or more

The game of "Jaws" requires a pool, a floating raft, and at least three players. One player is chosen to be the shark and the rest of the players climb on top of the floating raft. The shark tries to get the other players off the raft by any means possible. Once a player is knocked off the raft, he or she must get out of the water. The last player on the raft wins and gets to be the shark in the next round.

Marco Polo

Number of players: 2 or more

If you have access to a pool, your kids will love this fun game. Pick one child to be "it." This player will close his (or her) eyes and count to 10. Then, with eyes still closed, that player yells out "Marco". The other players must respond with "Polo" while swimming away. The child who is "Marco" must try to locate the other players by the sound of their voices and tag them. The last person to be caught can be the next "it." Feel free to substitute other word pairs for "Marco," and "Polo," to give this game a memorable twist.

Pillowcase Race

Number of players: 2 or more

Also fondly known as "Potato Sack Racing," this is a great outdoor game for both kids and adults. All you need is a large grassy area and an empty pillowcase for each player. Set a starting line and a finish line. Have all players line up at the starting line, standing inside their pillowcases and holding them up as high as possible. When a leader yells, "Go!" all the players must hop their way to the finish line. This is a hilarious game for the observers, as they watch their friends lose their balance and topple over one another. The first player to make it over the finish line in their pillowcase – and on their feet – is the winner.

Pool Categories

Number of players: 3 or more

This fun racing game requires a pool and at least three players. The player who is "it" stands on one side of a pool while the remaining players stand on the other. The "it" player decides on a category, such as colors, cereals, movies, etc. Once the category is chosen, the "it" player goes underwater while the remaining players pick a word in that category and speak it aloud. The "it" player then emerges from the water and starts to name things under their category.

For example, if the category is "colors," the player in the water might respond by saying, "Blue, green, yellow…" When players hear their chosen color they must race to the opposite side of the pool. The first player to reach the other side of the pool and call out the word they chose becomes the "it" player for the next round.

Twenty One Points

Number of players: 2 or more

It's also fun to play basketball with the family or a bunch of friends. You simply divide the group into even teams and then play against each other, abiding by the rules of a standard basketball game. The first team to reach 21 points is the winner.

Water Balloon Bombs

Number of players: 2 or more

This game is a lot of fun at an outdoor party, BBQ, or family reunion. It is most fun on a really hot summer day, as long as you don't mind getting your clothes wet. All you will need are some filled water balloons. You can stash your prepared ammo in a kiddie pool or a large cooler.

There are many ways to play with water balloons. In addition to unstructured play where you chase each other around the yard, lobbing balloons at anyone within range, here is a game that is simple, but fun.

Two players stand facing each other, a couple yards apart. The starting player selects a water balloon and tosses it to the other person, who catches it and throws it back. After a pair of successful catches, the players take a step backward. The goal is to see how far apart they can stand to pass the balloon before it breaks.

You can break large groups into teams of two players and go through a process of elimination. The last team standing the farthest from each other without breaking any water balloons wins.

Water Gun Battle

Number of players: 2 or more

If you find yourself on a hot summer afternoon with nothing much to do, why not load up some water guns and start a water gun battle? This can be an easy way to get in some exercise and cool down at the same time. There's nothing more fun than trying to avoid getting wet while trying to spray water on everyone else! It's a fun activity that all members of your family can enjoy.

Water Sports

Number of players: 2 or more

Almost any sport that is played on land can be played in the water, but basketball and volleyball are the most common. To play the water version of a sport, you can either invest a little money in special equipment, or you can use things you already have around the pool for your game. For water volleyball, you can hang a regular volleyball net above the middle of the pool or just string a line across the middle. You can make a basketball hoop out of a pool noodle, you can use a Nerf hoop and hang it over one end of the pool, or you can float an inner tube as a basket. An inner tube makes a challenging basket, because it floats around and doesn't stay in one place!

You can also use whatever water toys you already have to create suitable equipment for other water games. Pool noodles and a whiffle ball or a beach ball make for interesting water baseball, with bases marked as spots on the sides of the pool.

Just last weekend, my family and I went swimming and used a beach ball to play volleyball in the pool. We didn't have a real volleyball net so we placed the extendable pool skimmer across of the middle of the pool, laying it across the seats of two lawn chairs, one on either side of the pool.

Water Tag

Number of players: 2 or more

Here is a fun outdoor game if you have a large backyard and a long hose with a spray attachment. You will need at least two players for this game, although the more participants, the more fun. One player will operate the hose and try to eliminate each person by spraying water on the other players as they run away. The last person standing gets to operate the hose during the next round.

Chapter 2: Rainy Day Indoor Games

Outdoor play is great, but what about those days when the weather's nasty? What do you do during the long, cold winter months to burn off restless energy? Sure, you could play outside, but eventually, you'll start to feel the cold.

What do you do when night falls and your kids still have plenty of energy? This is where indoor play can come in especially handy! Although it can't be as physically stimulating as outdoor play, indoor play still has its value. It can help children develop their social and emotional skills, and can boost their imagination. It can also still count as exercise, because many indoor games still require some movement. In this chapter, you will discover the greatest indoor games that your child can play with other children or with adults.

Balloon Slap

This is a slow-motion version of volleyball that even young children can participate in. To play this game, you will need at least two players, some string and a balloon. Pick an area in your house where there is plenty of open space and remove any breakables. Attach the string from one wall to the other by taping the ends to the wall with masking tape or painter's tape. Fill a balloon with air and place at least one player on each side of the string. The goal of balloon slap is to have each player serve the balloon back and forth over the string without letting it hit the floor. The more players you have, the more balloons you can add to increase the challenge.

Board Game Night

Classic board games such a Life, Sorry, Monopoly, Candy Land, etc. never get old! Set aside a night as family board game night, where everyone gets to play with each other. A really cool idea is to provide snacks that are related to whatever game you're playing. For example, if you're playing Candy Land you could provide snacks like jolly ranchers, rock candy, ice cream sandwiches, chocolate pudding, etc.

You can have friends over for game night and make a variety of games available for them to play in different parts of the house. With snacks and something to drink, everybody can mingle, play the games that interest them, and generally have a good time.

Bouncy Ball Toss

Bouncy Ball Toss is a sort of hybrid, a mix of darts and inside basketball but much more challenging and exciting than straight basketball or darts by themselves. To play Bouncy Ball Toss, you will need some brown paper bags or empty containers, some small bouncy balls and a black marker. If you're using paper bags, you'll also need something to weigh down each bag.

To prepare for the game, use the black marker to write point values on each bag or container. You can then set up the containers in any configuration you'd like. I personally prefer a pyramid shape because it makes the game the most challenging, but you can arrange them in a line, in a geometric shape, or any way you choose. The objective is for each player to bounce the ball on the floor in such a way that it lands in one of the containers

To make the game even more challenging, you can try playing on different surfaces. Bouncy balls tend to bounce extra high on solid surfaces, which can give them an exhilarating velocity. Carpets tend to provide more of an aiming challenge because the balls won't bounce as high and often will take on interesting random tangents. You can also try playing on an uneven tile or gravel surface to see what happens.

You can also play this game on a flight of stairs if you don't have containers handy. In this formulation, players take turns throwing the bouncy ball toward the upper stair steps and counting the number of times it bounces before it hits the floor. I was an avid collector of bouncy balls when I was a child and often played this game on the stairs. Since then, I've taught the stairs version to my younger cousins who are five and three and they love it.

Creative Drawing

For this game, all you need is paper to draw on and anything you can draw with, from crayons to markers to pencils. In this game, one player begins by drawing something on the paper and passing it to the next person who can add to it. This game is quite fun in large groups because it's exciting to see what other players have added to the drawing by the time the paper gets back to you.

To keep everyone occupied, give each person a sheet of paper, so multiple drawings will be passed around the group, simultaneously. People can share colors, promoting cooperation, or be assigned a single color for the duration.

Family Bingo

This fun spin on bingo can hone your child's memory skills and is ideal for younger children who are still learning about their family members. All you will need is nine photos containing pictures of your family members and nine small objects that can serve as markers, such as buttons. Start by assembling the photos in a 3x3 square. Instead of calling out numbers, you call out names such as "Mom," or "Grandpa," and if the child has a photo of the family member you call, he or she places a marker on top until a line is created. You can play this game with any amount of children by just increasing the amount of photos you use by increments of nine. Playing with multiple players is fun because not everybody will have the same photos. This game is also fun for an older sibling to play with his or her younger siblings.

Floor Tile Checkers

Everyone is familiar with the time-tested game of checkers, but who says you need to go out and buy the official board game? If you have a floor in your home that has a pattern of squares, you can easily turn it into a giant checkerboard! All you will need is some masking tape and anything that can represent game pieces, such as small balls or rocks. This game is bound to entertain two little kids on a rainy day!

Use masking tape to mark off an area of the floor that will represent the board. You can then place a spot of tape through the middle of the "board" to designate each player's side. Using toys as designated game pieces, each child tries to get their pieces to the other player's side as in a traditional checkers game. You can alter the size of the "board" to suit your preferences, or to accommodate the size of the room. For younger children, you can start out with a smaller board to simplify the game while they learn it.

Go Fish

For this game, all you need is a deck of cards. Shuffle the deck and have one family member pass out seven cards to each player. Place the remaining cards in the middle. Everyone looks at their hands and pulls out any matching suits (the same card value; sevens, kings, etc.) to set on the table. One person starts the game by asking if anyone has a certain card. If nobody has that card value, the asker has to "go fish" by taking a card from the top of the deck, then the next player takes a turn. However many people have that card value, they are obliged to give it up to the player who asked, and that person gets to ask for another card. The first person to finish their hand by matching suits to all cards wins.

Homemade Connect the Dots

This game is ideal for toddlers and small youngsters who are still developing their fine motor skills. It's a great way for parents and their little ones to bond and have fun together. For this game, all you will need is a couple of large poster board sheets, a set of markers and some colorful circle-shaped stickers. You can make patterns on the poster board by placing the stickers strategically and the objective is for your toddler to use the marker to connect them. As your child grows or begins to master basic connecting

23

skills, you can make the objective more challenging by using different colored circle stickers and then encouraging your child to connect only the same-colored circles to build patterns that are more complex. It can also be fun to have your child try and guess what the final result will be based on where you've placed the stickers.

Indoors Bowling

This fun game is perfect for rainy days and is a cost-effective way to have some fun. Line up some empty water bottles in an open area, and then find a medium-sized, plastic ball. Take turns rolling the ball to knock down the water bottles as if they are bowling pins. If you need a foul line, lay down some masking tape or blue painter's tape; it's really easy to pull this up off the floor when you're done.

You can vary the difficulty by altering the size of the ball, by playing on carpet instead of hardwood, of by filling the bottles partway to make them harder to knock over.

Indoor Hoops

This game is a variant of basketball, only it's played indoors. The only equipment you need is something to serve as a ball and something you can use as a hoop. You can buy small balls and hoops meant for bedroom play, but I highly recommend being creative and using whatever materials you have at hand.

You can steal the office version of this game for home use. It consists of crumpled up balls of paper and a wastebasket as the hoop.

You can also use this game to encourage your kids to keep their room clean by using dirty clothes as the ball and a laundry basket as the hoop. To encourage your children to throw away their garbage, you can let them toss their empty cups, drink containers, plates, etc. into the garbage can.

Jigsaw Puzzles

Jigsaw puzzles are generally inexpensive, they can pose a good challenge, and can provide hours of relaxing enjoyment and good conversation. Puzzles are great for playing alone or with a few other friends. Jigsaw puzzles come in many designs. They range from the simple to the highly complex. I've even seen a 3D jigsaw puzzle that allows you to construct a castle.

Jigsaw puzzles can often be educational. One of the more popular designs is a map of the United States that is illustrated to represent what is unique about each state.

When children work on a jigsaw puzzle together, it encourages teamwork. Puzzles can become more exciting for small children, the closer they come to completion.

Name The Song

To play this game you will need some recorded music. This game is a great way to get children engaged in the world of music and share your favorite songs with them. One player, normally the parent, plays only a few seconds of a song. The objective is for the other player, normally the child (although it can be fun for the child and parent to switch roles), to guess what the song is, based on only listening to a few notes. This game can also be played between children. Whoever can guess the most songs correctly wins.

This can be a fun party game where everybody is asked to bring their favorite music and a way to play it. Players can take turns playing short clips of their favorite songs, increasing the clip length until someone guesses the song.

Old Maid

For this game, you will need a deck of cards with three queens taken out. The remaining queen is the "old maid" card. Once there is only one queen left in the deck, one person will deal out the entire deck evenly to the other players. After everyone has their cards, they go through their hands and lay down any matching suits.

The goal of the game is to make the most suits without being stuck with the "old maid" at the end of the hand. The players take turns, starting with the player to the left of the dealer, picking one card from the player to their left and setting aside their own matched suits. The hand ends when one player has no more cards.

The person left holding the "old maid" automatically loses the hand. The game can be played just for the fun of seeing who ends up with the "old maid", or you can keep score across several hands based on the number of suits each player has, excepting, of course, the player holding the "old maid" card.

Restaurant Memory

This is a fun game to play with the kids when you're out to eat at a restaurant. Most restaurants provide children under 12 with a cartoon-like menu or a placemat. After placing your orders, allow your child to study the images on the menu and ask them to memorize what they can. After a few minutes, take the menu, hold it in front of you and test your child(ren)'s memory by asking questions related to the menu such as, "How many tentacles does the octopus have?" or "How many bubbles is the cat blowing?" If you're playing with more than one child, you can keep track of how many points each person has and make the winner the first person to reach 20 points...or you could see who has the most points when the food arrives.

Silent Ball

This is a great game to play when parents need some peace and quiet. The players sit scattered around a room. The rules are that the players must pass a balled-up clean sock to each other but nobody can make a sound. If anyone makes noise, that person is out. Additionally, if a player can't catch the ball, that player is out, too. The game becomes the most fun when it gets down to the last two players who are competing hard to become the winner.

Spoons

Spoons can be a lot of fun and can result in a hilarious free-for-all. For this game you will need a deck of cards and one fewer spoons than you have players. Each player is dealt four cards and the remainder of the deck sits before the dealer. Place all the spoons (e.g., if you have five players, you will place four spoons) in the middle, with handles pointing outward. To begin the game, the dealer picks up one card from the deck, chooses one of the now five cards in the hand to discard, and passes the discard, face down to the player on his or her left. This player then selects a card to discard, handing it to the player on the left. The last player before the dealer, places his or her discard into a separate trash pile. The dealer continues to pick up a card and discard one to the left until the hand ends.

If you, as a player have amassed four of the same card, it is time to pick up a spoon. You can be sneaky and slip one away from the arrangement with nobody being the wiser, or you can brazenly grab one in the open. At any rate, you keep on passing cards around.

As soon as you, as a player, notice a spoon is missing, you may grab a spoon. What often results is a grand melee in which wrestling matches ensue, fingers are scratched, and spoons are bent. Ultimately, one person is left without a spoon, which means they get a letter, beginning with "S" and continuing on through "P", "O", "O", and "N". Once a player loses five hands, they are out of the game, along with one of the spoons. The cards are dealt again, the spoons are returned to the center, and play resumes. The game continues until, of the final two players, one is eliminated.

Stair Ball

Number of players: 1 or more

While we're talking about stairs, this is a wonderful way to play solo and have some fun in the process. Simply take a ball and bounce it against the upper stair steps. The objective is to keep the ball in play as long as possible by hitting it back up the stairs when it comes toward you. The ball remains in play until it hits the floor.

You can play this with friends by timing the amount of time the ball remains in play or by counting the number of hits before the ball hits the floor. The winner is the one with the longest playing time or the one with the most hits, depending on what rules you are using.

Sticky Ball

This fun indoor game is enjoyable for younger kids and promotes coordination skills. All you need is a roll of painter's tape or masking tape and paper that you don't mind crumpling up into balls (newspaper works great for this). Choose a wide doorway in your home and place pieces of tape, sticky side toward the players. You can place it in straight lines or create a web-like pattern. Then each player takes a turn throwing crumpled balls of paper at the tape in hopes that they will stick. Each stuck ball earns each player one point. The player with the most points after everyone has thrown their balls wins.

Thumb Wars

This has been a popular game among kids for many generations. It is a time-tested classic that promotes hand-eye coordination without the use of a television or a game controller. Thumb wars begins with two players, although kids often have tournaments to determine the champion of the group. Two players start by sitting, or standing, face to face and hooking their fingers around the other person's fingers in a firm grip that leaves the two thumbs sticking up. The objective of Thumb Wars is to use your own thumb to pin down your opponent's thumb. Once you've got your opponent's thumb in your grasp, you must keep it down while you count out loud to three before the victory becomes yours.

Tic Tac Toe

This fun two-person game only requires something to write with and something to write on. To begin with, one player draws a three by three square grid. The other player marks an "X" in a box. The first player marks an "O" in another box. The two players take turns marking a box at a time in an attempt to get three of the same symbol in a row, whether vertically, horizontally, or diagonally. The first player to get three in a row draws a line through it and yells "tic tac toe!" For a fun variation, you can switch up the symbols to be anything you want. Fun ideas include smiley faces, animals, shapes, etc

Chapter 3: Group Games

Team-sized games can be the most fun of them all! Many of these games can be adapted for inside play, which gives them flexibility for all sorts of events, including birthday parties, family reunions, school fairs, and potlucks. You can use them for a "non-event" too, such as when you find your house full of youngsters and need to come up with something to do, and fast! The games I've included in this chapter can be enjoyed by children of all ages and are great for times when you need to add a little pizzazz to your life.

Because these games are performed in groups, they present an ideal opportunity to develop crucial social skills and teamwork. Team-building games help enhance one's morale, develop latent leadership, experiment with creativity, and grow together in the ability to effectively solve problems. However, that's no reason to imagine that they fall short in the fun category. As I said, group games can be the most fun of them all!

Charades

In this fun acting game, one child picks a word or phrase and then acts it out with gestures so that the other kids can work to guess it. No verbal cues are allowed in this game; only body language, facial expressions, and gestures. The person who guesses the right word or phrase gets to act out the next one. This is a fun game for adults as well as mixed-age groups.

Cheese Puff Blow

To play Cheese Puff Blow, you will need masking tape, a bag of cheese puffs, one straw for each player, and enough players to split into at least two teams. If you want to add up points, you can place a hand-drawn target labeled with point values, at the finish line. You'll also need to clear a table for this game or, I suppose, you could play on a floor space.

The players should break into teams of two people each. You can use masking tape to mark the start and finish lines at opposite ends of the table. Beyond the finish line, you can tape down the target. Each team picks one player to face off against the other team. Both players should set a cheese puff behind the starting line. When an appointed player says, "Go!" both players should blow through their straws to move their cheese puff toward the finish line. When the first cheese puff rolls across the finish line, both players stop blowing and let it roll onto the target itself. The first team to earn 20 points is the winner.

Dice Roll

To play this simple yet fun game, all you will need is a die or pair of dice and one piece of paper for each player. Each player takes a turn rolling the dice and records each number they roll. The object of the game is to add the numbers together and be the first person to reach 100. As players approach 100, the competitive side sometimes really comes out!

Draw and Fold

Draw and fold requires a minimum of four players, a pen or pencil for each person, and one piece of paper for each round. It is best if everyone sits in a circle. To start, the first player writes a sentence at the top of the paper and then passes it to the player on their right. The second player then rewrites the sentence but in the form of drawings. For example, if player number one wrote "I love you," then player number two could draw two stick figures with a heart in between them. The second player then folds the top of the paper so that the written sentence is hidden and only their illustration is visible before passing it to the third player. The third player then must try and decipher the drawing by translating it into a written sentence and folding the paper to hide the drawing. Player four then must try and translate the new sentence into a new drawing. Players keep passing the paper around until either the paper is used up or the circuit is completed. At the end, everyone can look at the entire piece of paper to reveal all of the answers. Like Telephone, the final results can often be hilarious.

Family Jeopardy

Does your family love trivia questions? If so then this could be a perfect game to play at family events. To prepare for this game, you will write up questions and answers about your family beforehand. Questions may include things such as, "What year did Sally graduate from college?" or "What is Dad's middle name?" You can break the questions into categories as they do in the actual Jeopardy show, and categorize them by family member or by theme. You should also assign a point value to each question. Depending on the size of your family and the age of the participants, each person can play individually or work as part of a team. After all of the questions are exhausted, the person or team with the most points wins.

Freeze Dance

This delightful game can be played solo or with a group of friends. Pick some fun music. The rule is that everyone must stop dancing when the music is turned off, no matter what position they are in. If a player moves or falls out of position, he's out.

Design a playlist that includes the most popular kids' songs. If you have some energetic children, this is a good way to wear them down. Freeze dance can also be played using chairs scattered around the room(one fewer than the number of participants), as a fun tweak to musical chairs.

When the music stops, everyone scrambles for a seat and the person left without one is eliminated. Before each round you will take a chair away until there is only one left, and whoever gets that last seat when the music stops is the winner.

Guess the Drawing

This game requires large pieces of paper and some markers. Hang up blank sheets of white paper on the wall. One player goes up to the paper and starts to draw something while the rest of the players yell out guesses as to what the drawing is. Whoever can guess the right word first gets to be the next person to draw a word.

This can be easily turned into a team game by giving the artist for each team the same word. The team that guesses the word first wins a point for the team and another artist for each team is chosen for the next round.

Hot Potato

For this game, put on some fun music and pass around a light object, like a beanbag or a small ball. Whoever has the object in hand when the music is turned off is "out." When it's down to two people, the person without the "hot potato" when the song ends is the winner..

Human Twist Puzzle

In this fun teambuilding game, all participants stand in a circle. The ideal size for this activity is about nine people, so if you have a large bunch of people who want to play, you may want to divide them into smaller groups.

At any rate, instruct the players to walk forward and grasp the right hand of the person in the opposite side of the circle. When everyone has accomplished this step, ask them to clasp the left hand of somebody near them.

This will result in everyone connected in a snarled mass. The objective of this game is to work together to untangle the mess without letting go of anyone's hand. When solved, the participants should be once more in a circle, holding hands.

As you can imagine, this game requires some close physical contact. Depending on the age of the participants, some people may be most comfortable in a same-sex group, and others may not be comfortable with any physical contact at all, so stay sensitive to the needs of your guests. Generally, if your participants would be comfortable playing the game "Twister" they'll have no problem with this activity.

I Would Rather

This game is a good icebreaker, because it helps young children discover others with whom they have things in common. All you need for this game is a list of questions. Each question should require the players to choose between two options and to show their choice by moving to a designated side of the room. All players begin by walking to the center of the room. For example, if the question is, "Would you rather wear a baseball cap or a visor?" you would designate one side of the room for visors and the other side for those who prefer baseball caps. This can continue with a few more questions that are hand-crafted to help kids learn more about each other.

Improv Skits

This game is great for a large group of people and it goes over well with mixed-age groups. Preparation is fairly simple; just fill a few paper bags with random items from your house. Include a mix ranging from articles of clothing to kitchen utensils to anything in your rec room that you don't mind people handling. Divide the participants into groups of around six people and give each group a bag of random items. Give each group a few minutes to design a short skit using each of the items in the bag; then come back together to watch each other's skits. Hint: the more random the items in a bag, the funnier each skit is bound to be.

Mummy Wrapping Contest

This fun game requires at least two players who are willing to be mummies and at least four players who are willing to break into teams and race to wrap their mummy. The only equipment required is a roll of toilet paper for each team. Each mummy stands still while the teams use an entire roll of toilet paper in a race to wrap their mummy the fastest. Keep a camera handy to snap some funny photos.

Simon Says

"Simon Says" is another classic game that kids love. Pick one child to be "Simon." That child will then call out commands, most of the time starting with the words, "Simon says." For example, one command might be "Simon says touch your nose." If "Simon" does not start the command with those two key words and a player performs the command anyway, he or she is out.

One variation of this game that is loved by younger children is to replace the name "Simon," with the name of the person who is in charge of giving the commands. Kids love the idea and it is sure to generate some laughs and giggles from the crowd.

Stick Dance

This game requires an odd number of players, some music and a long stick, a broom, or a yardstick. Each player picks a dancing partner. The odd man out (or woman) dances with the stick. Somebody not participating in the game will be in charge of turning the music on and off. The music player starts the music and lets everybody dance with their partner for a few seconds before stopping it. When the music stops, everybody must stop dancing and switch partners. The player who is left without a partner must then dance with the stick until the music stops again.

Team Story Telling

The point of this activity is to gather all the participants together and let each player take a turn at adding to a story line. For example, the first player will start off by creating the first sentence – or phrase – of a story. It can literally be anything. The next player will then add a second sentence or phrase to the story. Go around the group, letting each person contribute a part, until the story is wrapped up by the last player.

The game can become unwieldy and people may lose interest if there are too many people. If you have more than a dozen people, I recommend you split up into separate groups and let each group develop a separate story. The story can be played out loud or it can be written down a sentence at a time on a piece of paper and passed from person to person, to be read out loud at the end. Players can be highly creative, leaving the story hanging after introducing an unusual phrase.

To add to the level of difficulty, have each participant write the name of a person, a place, or an object on separate pieces of paper. Then mix up the paper and have each person draw an item to use as part of their contribution to the story.

Telephone

This fun game is good for when kids are together in groups of at least five. The first child or adult thinks of a phrase and then whispers it into the next player's ear. That player then whispers it into the next player's ear. The last player speaks the phrase aloud to see if it matches the original phrase. Sometimes the phrase gets so mashed up that the end result is hilarious. This was another fun game that I played as a child, and a few times I took great pleasure in changing the phrase purposely causing the whole class to laugh at the end.

The "Egg-cellent" Race

This awesome party game is great for events with large groups of people. All that is required is enough spoons for each player and one egg per team. If you're playing outside, it's a lot of fun to play with raw eggs. However, if you're playing indoors, I suggest you boil the eggs; otherwise it has the potential to get messy. Begin by dividing the group into teams.

This is a relay race, so half the group should be on one side of the field and half on the other side. The two sides should be about ten feet apart. The first person to play begins the race with the handle of their spoon in their mouth and an egg in the spoon. The race begins with that player balancing the egg while racing across to the other side and transferring the egg into the next player's spoon. If the egg drops or breaks, then the team is eliminated. The first team to complete all legs of the race with egg intact is the winner.

Treasure Hunt

What can be more fun and challenging than searching for "buried treasure?" For this game, hide an object or a set of objects somewhere around the house and leave clues. You can start out by leaving the clues in obvious places and then have each clue lead your child to the next hidden spot. You can also draw a map and have your child find the treasure that way. This game can also be fun when played outdoors. If the group is large, you may want to group the players into teams, giving each team a different set of clues, or at least scramble the order of the clues.

The Human Christmas Tree

This is a great family game to play around Christmas or Thanksgiving time and is guaranteed to cause some laughs. Keep a camera ready to take pictures.

For this game, all you will need are some Christmas-themed arts and crafts materials, such as leftover wrapping paper, stickers, tissue paper, or ribbons. One person volunteers to serve as the "tree" while the other players take turns using the material to "dress" the tree. If you're throwing a birthday party, you could play the game using birthday party materials to "wrap" a "present". There is no competitive objective to this game, so it can generate some silliness and create great memories for years to come.

Umbrella Ball

For this game, you will need a large umbrella and a couple of large bouncy balls. Open the umbrella and place it upside down on the ground. Have each player stand 5 to 10 feet away and try to bounce their ball into the umbrella. Every time a player successfully gets a ball to stay in the umbrella, a point is scored. Anyone who causes the umbrella to tip over and spill out the balls, loses all points and starts again.

Chapter 4: Solo Games

Sometimes there's just nobody around to play games with. This chapter is dedicated to games that a child – or an adult, for that matter - can play alone. Parents or guardians can also participate in these solo games, which is great for building parent-child relationships. My Dad and I used to spend many weekends together, just the two of us, but we always found something to do together for entertainment. This chapter offers some great games that your child can play alone or with you.

Bubble Gum Challenge

This game can be played with one child or as a race between multiple children. All you need is some wrapped bubble gum, preferably a hard-to-chew variety, and a pair of oven mitts, socks or anything the children can fit over their hands. The Bubble Gum Challenge is to see how long it takes to unwrap the piece of gum, chew it, and blow a bubble.

Guess the Hand

This classic and simple game is popular among small children and can help them develop the ability to recognize visual cues. Player one is the parent and player two is the child. To play guess the hand, all you need do is hide a small object in your hand by balling your fist, then ask your child to guess which hand is hiding the object.

Home-Made Skee Ball

Who doesn't love the classic game of skee ball? Instead of packing the family up for a trip to the ever-so-expensive arcade, here's how to easily make a free home version using only a cardboard box and an empty egg container:

Your box should ideally be square and have four flaps. Using a safety knife, remove the four flaps and then cut the top of the box at an upwards angle. Tape the four flaps together and then attach it to the bottom angle of the box using some tape. Place an empty egg carton inside of the box to serve as the ball catcher. It may be helpful to glue the egg carton to the floor of the box so it won't move around or get lost. Using some small, lightweight balls (bouncy balls do the trick and can also be used for some of the other games in this book), each player takes turns tossing a ball up the ramp with the objective of getting all of their balls into the egg carton!

Hopscotch

Hopscotch is a great solo game and can also be played outdoors to promote physical activity. It can be played by children as young as four or five. The first step is to draw a grid. If you're playing outside, you can draw squares on the sidewalk with a piece of chalk. If you're playing indoors, you can use masking tape to mark out the squares on the floor. The most common hopscotch pattern is a single square, followed by two squares side by side, then one square followed by two squares, but you can make it however you'd like. One option is to place different numbers inside each square.

The player begins by throwing a small object such as a rock into the first square. The rock must land completely inside. The player then starts to hop through the course, landing on one foot for single squares and two feet for double squares. Once the player reaches the end, he or she turns and hops back, grabbing the rock along the way. Then he or she tosses the rock into the next square and repeats the pattern. If the player steps on one of the lines or outside of the squares, he or she must start over. To make this game more challenging, you can add variations to the rules. For example, you could set a rule to skip over the square holding the marker.

How Fast Can You Go?

An only child can turn almost any everyday task into a fun game by turning it into a timed challenge. Challenge your child to see how long it takes him or her to dress, to wash the dishes, to take out the garbage, to pick up their room or any other task that would otherwise be viewed as a boring chore. Turning chores into games can help your child gain competitive skills and inspire him or her to strive for improvement.

Ice Digger

The objective of ice digger is to free a small treasure from a small block of ice using only the materials provided. To prepare for this game, take a disposable cup and place a small non-floating item in it before filling the cup with water. Once the water is completely frozen, you can then pop out the ice or peel the disposable cup away to reveal the block of ice. Provide your child with tools such as a small amount of hot water, a spoon to chip away the ice or anything you can think of to help them unbury the frozen treasure. Unless you're playing this outdoors, it can be helpful to let them work on their ice over a shallow pan so the water doesn't get all over the place.

Magic Cup Game

You've probably seen this age-old game before. The best part about it is that the amount of players who can participate is versatile. An adult can play it with one to three small children, up to four small children can play it amongst themselves, or a child can challenge him or herself by playing it alone. Take three plastic cups and put a small item underneath one, preferably something like a coin or a small stone. Then shuffle the cups around and have the participants guess which one contains the item.

If you are playing with a group of children, you use sleight of hand to switch items when a kid starts to catch on. You can also help them learn the game so they can trick their friends. Almost any magic book can help you learn this trick.

Make Your Own Puzzle

Here is another really fun and time-tested game. Let your child draw a picture and then cut it up into puzzle pieces that can be easily reassembled. You can cut it into easy squares and triangles or you can get really challenging and cut it into crazy shapes. You can also cut up pictures from magazines or newspapers to make an interesting puzzle. My dad used to make up puzzles for me when I was little and I was often entertained for hours by them.

Solitaire

Solitaire is a legendary single-player card game that can be played with a deck of cards and is available as a free game on most computer systems. To begin, shuffle a standard deck of cards and divide it into seven stacks. Set the stacks face down from left to right, then begin to flip cards face up as follows. The first row should only contain a single card, face up. The second row should contain two cards, one face up one face down, the third row will have three cards, one face up and two face down, and so on. The seventh row should contain seven cards in the same fashion. Place the leftover cards to the side to draw from. The goal of Solitaire is to build each row from Ace to King in the same suit with every card alternating in color. The YouTube video Solitaire Games: Solitaire Card Game Rules by eHowSports offers additional visual insight on how to play this game.

Solve a Rubik's Cube

A Rubik's Cube is a small, adjustable cube that has a different color on each of its six faces. Each face consists of smaller squares that can be moved by turning the sides of the cube. The object of this game is to start with the colors scrambled and then return it to solid colors on each side of the cube. This is the only game I've included that is necessary to buy, but it is widely available in any store that sells games or toys.

The Box Game

For this game, you will need a small lightweight cardboard box. Empty macaroni boxes work well. The objective of the game is to pick the box off the floor using your teeth and without holding onto anything for support. You can play this game alone or you can include the whole family. It's fun and entertaining to see who can pick the box up most successfully. If this game is too easy, you can create variations, such as picking it up with your teeth while standing on one leg.

The Sensory Game

This game is geared for small children and is often best played with a parent. You will need a bag filled with random items from around the house. The child, with closed eyes, reaches into the bag, grabs an item and then attempts to guess what it is by using the other senses. Older kids may be bored with this game but it can be exciting for little children.

Towering

Building a tower out of random items can be fun and an entertaining challenge, both for you and for any lookers-on. You can play on your own or with friends. I sometimes, even now, can be caught building a tower out of the items on my table, while I wait for my food at a restaurant.

You can use items with a variety of weights, sizes, shapes, and textures and see how high you can build your tower. Small children often can be entertained for hours with things like paper cups, building blocks, cardboard boxes or books. You can use virtually any solid substance as part of your tower.

Playing cards are by far the most challenging material to use because they are so light and glossy. When I was little, I used to stack the little individual creamers containers and see how high I could go before it toppled over.

If you decide to play a towering game with multiple participants, players can break up into teams or play individually. Whoever's tower is the highest or stands the longest is the winner.

Wall Ball

If you like to practice your catching skills, wall ball is a fun game that you can play solo, or with others. All you need is a wall and a ball that bounces. Tennis balls usually work well. Simply throw the ball against the wall and then catch it when it bounces back. Throwing the ball hard can create an exciting challenge.

Chapter 5: Educational Games

Who says all games are just for fun? Or that learning can't be fun? Games can provide an effective way for everyone, from the youngest children to oldest adults to sharpen important physical and mental skills that will help them both in school and when it comes to "real" life. Almost all of the games we've already discussed require some sort of learning or skill development. Here's a summary of some of the benefits you can gain from the games we've already talked about:

Game Title	Chapter	Developmental Focus				
		Hand-eye Coord.	Memory	Balance	Social	Problem Solving
Ball Race	1	▓				
Balloon Slap	2			▓		▓
Basketball Games	1					▓
Board Games	2		▓			
Bouncy Ball Toss	2	▓				
Box Game	4	▓			▓	
Bubble Gum Challenge	4	▓				
Card Games	2					▓
Charades	3				▓	▓
Cheese-Puff Blow	3	▓				
Coin Toss	1			▓		
Connect the Dots	2	▓	▓			
Creative Drawing	2	▓			▓	

Game	#					
Dice Roll	3	▓				
Draw and Fold	3	▓				
Egg-cellent Race	3	▓			▓	
Family Bingo	2					▓
Family Jeopardy	3	▓				
Floor Tile Checkers	2		▓		▓	▓
Football Fortune	1	▓				
Four Square	1	▓				
Freeze Dance	3					▓
Guess the Drawing	3				▓	
Guess the Hand	4		▓			▓
Hide and Seek	1		▓			▓
Hopscotch	4				▓	
Hot Potato	3				▓	
How Fast?	4	▓				
Human Christmas Tree	3		▓			
Human Twist	3					
I Would Rather	3	▓				
Ice Digger	4				▓	▓
Indoor Hoops	2		▓			
Indoor Bowling	2		▓			
Jaws	1	▓				▓

Game						
Magic Cup	4		X		X	
Marco Polo	1	X				
Mummy Wrapping	3					X
Name the Song	2	X				
Outdoor Sports	1					X
Pillow Case Race	1				X	
Pool Categories	1				X	
Puzzles	2					X
Sensory Game	4				X	X
Silent Ball	2					X
Simon Says	3				X	
Skee Ball	4	X				
Skits	3	X				
Solitaire	4				X	
Stair Ball	2				X	
Stick Dance	3				X	X
Sticky Ball	2	X				
Story Telling	3	X				X
Tag	1	X				X
Telephone	3					X
Thumb Wars	2	X				
Tic Tac Toe	2	X				X
Towering	4					X
Treasure Hunt	3	X				

Umbrella Ball	3					
Wall Ball	4					
Water Balloon Bombs	1					
Water Gun Battle	1					
Water Tag	1					

Games can help children – and adults, too – increase their skills in spelling, vocabulary, sentence formation, math, geography, motor skills and social interaction. Most kids already learn by watching educational television shows and playing video games. Sometimes a simple game can be used to teach children valuable skills that can help them keep their brains sharp. They can help adults, too, by keeping their skills honed and their brains functioning optimally.

Alphabet Categories

You can play this game with only one child or with a group of children. It can also be great fun to play with individuals of mixed ages. One player picks a broad category, such as cars, animals, or television shows. The first player names five of anything that falls in that category and starts with the letter "A." The second player then does the same, using the letter "B." Players continue to take turns down the letters of the alphabet until someone gets stuck. They then can change to a different category and start over.

Card Memory

The object of this game is to test one's memory and concentration skills. It can be played solo or with multiple players. One player shuffles a deck of cards and then lays each card out face down in a square grid pattern. Each player takes turns flipping over two cards of his or her choice. If the cards are a matching pair, the player gets to keep the cards and turns over another pair of cards.

If the cards are *not* a matching pair, all members try to remember what they are; then the cards are turned face down again, and the next player takes a turn. The game continues until all pairs have been matched. The player with the most cards at the end is the winner.

Color Cars

This is a fun game to play when you're riding in the car with your kids. It also helps younger kids learn about colors and counting. Before taking off on an errand, each player picks a color and then guesses how many cars of that color he or she will see on the way to your destination. Each player is responsible for keeping count of how many cars he or she sees in the color he or she picked. The player with the highest count when you reach your destination is the winner. On a long road trip you can divide this game into smaller intervals of 10 minutes, or stop when someone has seen, say, 20 cars in a single color.

General Trivia

Trivial Pursuit is a well-known and popular board game that tests the overall knowledge of its players. However, if you don't own the game, you can easily do a quick online search that yields thousands of trivia questions with answers and use them to make your own version for friends and family to play.

One sixth-grade teacher prepares 10 questions and then asks his students to write down their answers to each question on a sheet of lined paper. Afterwards, they review the answers together to see who got the most right. This can be a fun party game as well, with prize trinkets for the people who have the most correct answers.

Hangman

This simple game, requiring only something to write with and something to write on, is a great way to learn words. One player secretly selects a word and then writes out one space for each letter in the word. The other player has to guess the word by randomly guessing individual letters. If the letter belongs in the word, then the first player writes the letter in the blanks where it occurs. If the player picks a letter that is not in the word, the other player will draw a body part on the hangman. If the hangman is complete and the word is not completely spelled out, the game is lost.

This game can go on for quite a while, depending on how detailed you want to get with your hangman. Some kids like to keep it basic by ending with a head, body, two arms and two legs but you can keep the game going as long as you want by adding fingers, hair, shoes, clothes etc.

I Spy and I Rhyme

This game is similar to the traditional "I Spy" game but has a little bit of an educational twist. The goal of I spy and I rhyme is to find an object in the room that rhymes with the object the previous player has chosen. For example, if player one says "I spy a book," then player two may say "I spy a hook" or "I spy a nook."

License Plate Addition

This fun math game can be played while driving or while taking a walk around a neighborhood that has many parked cars. One player looks at a license plate number and then calls out the numbers that are on it. Most license plates contain two to three numbers. The first player who can correctly add those numbers wins. With higher-skilled players, you can add numbers of two or three digits together or multiply single digits.

Step School

If you have a staircase in your house you can try playing "step school." The bottom step is considered the lowest grade possible and the highest step is the highest education possible. Everyone starts at the bottom step and an older child or adult serves as the teacher. The teacher asks each person a question and the difficulty is based on what step that player is on. If a player is on the lowest step, the teacher would ask an easy question such as "What is 1+1?" and then asks increasingly harder questions. Whoever can make it to the top step first is the winner.

The States Game

This is another great game that can be played almost anywhere and it is also very educational. One member of the family starts out by picking a state. The next player has to name a state that starts with the last letter of that state. If Mom picks Georgia, Dad might pick Alaska, Junior might pick Arkansas, and so on. You can also do this for cities, colors, etc.

Traveling Word Alliterations

This game is great for stimulating the minds of little ones and teaching them about word alliteration. The goal of the game is for each player to imagine that he or she will be taking a trip somewhere and will have to bring something that starts as the same letter as their destination. For example, a player can say "I'm traveling to Florida and bringing my Fish," or "I'm traveling to Cousin Charlie's and bringing my Crayons." To make the game more fun, encourage creativity and silliness.

War

This fun card game requires a deck of cards and at least two players. It can help children learn the order of numbers and their relative values.

One player shuffles the deck of cards and deals the entire deck out face down. Once each player has a pile of cards, all players flip over their top card. Whoever has the card with the highest number wins all the cards. For example, if one player flips over a 10 and the second player flips over a three, the first player, having the highest point value, would collect both cards. If both players pull a matching number, each player draws three cards, keeping them facedown and then flips over the fourth card. Whoever has the highest-valued card gets all of the cards. The first player to collect all of the cards is the winner.

For young children just learning their numbers, it's easiest to remove the face cards (the king, queen, jack and ace) and just stick with the numbers.

Word Association

This game requires at least two players, although the more participants, the more potential you have for hilarity. Player one starts by saying any word they like. The second player then says the first thing that comes to mind upon hearing the word. Any additional players then follow suit, responding to the word that was said by the previous player.

A word cannot be used twice in one game. For example, if player one says, "dog," player two could say, "hair," and player three could say "brush," and player four could say "teeth", but "hair" could not be repeated. The further you can carry the associations the funnier they will be, because you eventually start running out of words and find yourself challenged to use words more creatively.

Word and Number Puzzles

Crossword puzzles have been played for at least a century and Sudoku puzzles have gained popularity in the last few years. Both games are mentally stimulating. You can readily find online a variety of these puzzles that vary in level of difficulty, to accommodate the skill levels of the players. Some people will work together to solve a puzzle, while others prefer to work alone. Crosswords and word search puzzles can provide great bonding times for children with the adults in their lives.

21 Questions

One player thinks of a well-known person and the rest of the players have to ask yes or no questions to narrow down the possibilities. The object of the game is to see if anyone can guess the name of the individual in less than 21 questions. Sometimes the challenge can be difficult and everyone has a fun time guessing. This game can be played anywhere. My dad and I used to play it during long road trips and it really tested my knowledge. It's also quiet enough to play in restaurants or waiting rooms and can be used to distract children from a dreaded appointment.

Conclusion

I hope this book was able to help you to discover some fun and educational games that you can play together in your household, share with friends and let your kids share with their friends. Games are a great source of relaxation, fun, and laughter. They can build amazing memories. Play is important to help young minds and bodies develop essential skills from coordination and balance to communication and problem solving. Active games increase body awareness and imagination. They can be played indoors, outdoors, with friends and family, in the car, at school, and alone.

Research shows that families who regularly play games together get along better. Cherished family memories can find their birth in family game nights. While the common conception is that fewer families are spending time together today, research shows that they are actually spending *more* time together than ever before. The key difference, however, is that families are not spending as much *quality* time together. Incorporating a family activity night into your schedules can help to promote quality time together.

Your next step is to test out some of the games you discovered here. It may take some trial and error, but if you keep at it, you can discover what activities work best for your family, your children, and their friends.

Begin by planning your very own family or friend game night. The most important detail to decide is where and when to schedule it. I recommend setting aside a regular time with the agreement of others. A family game night will be more likely to be successful if you solicit the input of each member of the family. If your children are mature enough to take charge of the games, you can rotate the responsibility or, at the very least, include games that are favorites of most everybody.

Next, think about times, such as a family reunion or holiday, when your extended family gets together. What activities can you incorporate that will make the time memorable and enjoyable? You'll want to consider who you think will participate in playing. It is important to include at least some games that everyone, from the littlest toddler to the most aged grandparents, can enjoy together.

The initial planning may be a little challenging, but you may well be generating priceless memories that will last long in the minds of your family members. Here again, let other people share in the planning if they wish. The more people who take an active part in the preparation, the more others will be likely to participate and invite others to join in the fun. I hope you and your friends and family have many incredible hours of gaming entertainment!

Thanks for reading.

If this book helped you or someone you know in any way, then please spare a few moments right now to leave a nice review.

My Other Books

Be sure to check out my author page at:
https://www.amazon.com/author/susanhollister

UK: http://amzn.to/2qiEzA9

Or simply type my name into the search bar: Susan Hollister

Thank You

26817865R00034

Printed in Great Britain
by Amazon